Poetry's Love Song

BY ARISTON CM

Poetry's Love Song

ARISTON C.M.

Published by Midnight Fire Ministries INC.

I lovingly dedicate this book to a very important person in my life, Q. Lemon.

You have made a world of difference in my life. You have taught me what love should look and feel like. You have taught me what it is to be a friend. Thank you for understanding who I am.
Nothing for me will ever be the same.

You are a blessing to me, I love you and I will always be thankful for you.

Introduction

For centuries poetry has been used to convey emotions and used as a creative way of communication. In this book I am sharing my heart and the heart of many others. It is no secret that love rests at the fiber of everything we are. Love can sometimes hurt, even though it is not meant to. At some point in all our lives we will all experienced pain from someone who says they love us. Although it doesn't feel good at the moment, we can learn valuable lessons from it. Yes, it hurts, then it changes us; often it is for the better, in some cases it's worse. I've learned you haven't experienced anything until you have experienced love. Love is many things, but it's not always what you think it is, so you have to understand love in order to embrace it. At some point in all our lives we need love. No matter how much we say we don't, we do. Love is who all of us are, but experiences have damaged our outlook on love and intimate relationships. This book contains a mix of emotions that connects to love; some good, some bad, and some that will give us hope. Hope that we will truly find the love that satisfy our thirsty souls. This book contains some of the poetry from my book *The Courage to Dance Again: Finding Purpose in Your Pain.* It is my hope that you will enjoy the full range of emotions that you will feel as a result of reading this book. May you find love and satisfaction in all areas of your life. Embrace the beauty of love, it has been waiting for you!

Someone Beautiful

I met someone beautiful
He brought me back to life
He held the keys to my journey
He changed my whole life
He taught me to live
And how to be free
To put myself first
And how to focus on loving me
He is a gem
A precious rare find
I can only selfishly hope
That somehow, someday
He will kinda be mine
He has to live, learn and grow
I can't limit time
I must allow it to go slow
Failure to adhere
To the given design
Will cancel our purpose
And altar time
I met someone beautiful
It was supposed to be
I can tell I will love him
And forever be free.

Private Thoughts

Lord, you already know
I don't know what's happening
Maybe this is part of my growth
It's not your will that I suffer
But I suffer so
I can't be held accountable for the things I don't know
I'm following the plan
I have put it all in your hands
You see my broken weary soul
When will you put it back together
My faith is growing old
Open my eyes that I may see
What I am missing
Or is it really me
It seems you're withholding love
Why? when you've made this the biggest part of me
Am I to give
But never receive
Oh, what torture
How can I continue to live?
I'm decaying inside
I'm emaciated
I have no choice but to hide
I have no pride
My crown has been taken
I've been dethroned

There is nothing left
My private thoughts
Are all that I own

When A Man Loves A Woman

When a man loves a woman
      It's unlike anything you have ever seen
There's no need to carry out your wildest dreams
      His fire for you burns deep within
In place that no one has ever been
      His heart longs for you
In his mind he adores you
      He exists for you
And all his love
      Has been saved only for you
You'll never doubt
      That his love is true
When a man loves a woman
      She feels safe and secure
No worries when he walks out the front door
      Her heart is soft
And her love is gentle
      Unguarded emotions that transcend into him
Vulnerable
Moldable
Look what good love can do
When a man loves a woman
      It's unlike anything you've ever seen
It is better than the best dream you have ever dreamed
When a man loves a woman
      Her soul is set free

Summer lasts forever

And dawns never cease

Bliss

Unmeasurable happiness
        Characterized by love
The sun always shines
        The peacefulness of dusk
Settles on your insides
        The wind gently blows
And whispers in your ear
        Laughter is forever
Passionate love fills the air
        It's so intense
That you can hardly bear
        Dark sweet nights
Covered in chocolate
        Kissed with Carmel
What a delight
        The place where happiness is free
And the expectations are light
        Bliss, the place where
Fantasy starts and
Love never ends

Forever Beautiful

Forever beautiful you are

       Yes, you are to me

Your light brown eyes

       That dimple on the side

Rare beauty

Perfection

       Not from man's design

Your smell

Your touch

So much finesse

       I treasure you so much

       Forever beautiful you are to me

Without your love

       I'm not complete

As darkness is to the moon

       So is your love to me

Forever beautiful

       My darling, you are to me

Tranquility My Love

Tranquility my love
     I impart myself to you
I rest well, but only when inside of you
     Embrace me, make me fall in love with you
I promise to care deeply
     And reserve my love only for you
Let me caress
     Your mind, body, and soul
With me you'll stay youthful
     And never grow old
My life is in your hands
     With me you're in control
I come with no demands
     Please know that you're safest
While nestled in my hands
     I will help you deal with life's demands
I want to be your soul mate
     And help you be all you can be
Connect with me
     Tranquility
My love you will always be

Love Is A Choice

When I look into your eyes I see promise
  Hope and fulfillment
The promise of a better life
  The hope that all dreams will come true
  And the fulfillment that comes with
  Everlasting love.
I then ask myself a question, how can I
  Fit into the simple world of you?
Where happiness is not based of life's circumstances
  And love is free
There is a sweet innocence shared between you and me
  One that I want to last all eternity
All that you're made of I cannot see
  But in time God will reveal it to me
As we grow in life and love, we'll take
  Direction from our father up above
Our togetherness defies all time and space
  It breaks all boundaries set from within
Could it be your stillness or warm embrace
  That captures me day after day
As I move into a deeper understanding of
  Life, I learn that love is a choice and
  It sometimes chooses you

Just For You

I've been going through some things that have threatened to
take me away
I cried to the Lord and I heard him say
For I know the plans I have for you, thus saith the Lord
let me start
I'm not going to just let any man have your heart
You see there's a reason you've been divorced two times
You're trying to do this on your own
Not realizing you're mine
I know your heart
I see your pain
I see how you walk around each and every day
I know you think he's beautiful
And this may be true
But is he really the one that I have prepared for you
I examine the heart
And judge the things you don't see
Sometimes beauty is only skin deep
Who is man to take ownership of your heart
It's fragile, each and every part
Trust me on this one
You have so much to gain

But you must be patient
Quit searching
I already know his name
You will too when I'm done with you
I love you
And I'm saving the best, just for you

The Promise

I waited for you
       But you never came
You weren't there during my time of pain
       Our hearts were connected
Our souls were as one
       Our love was full of energy similar to the sun
You promised me forever
       You said I was the one
The promise soon faded
       It burned like the noonday Sun
With only memories to hold me at night
       I constantly think what would life with you be like
The plans we made
       The dreams we shared
I looked for you
       You weren't there
My heart grew faint
       My soul became tired
I soon realized you took the promise
       And left me with desire

Mommy

Today you choose to take my life
    Mommy, think, isn't there something else
You could have sacrificed?
    You ended my life so that you
Could live yours.
    What did I do to deserve this?
I haven't been born
    Did you make this decision based on
My best interest?
    Couldn't be, it must be based on yours
Where's my dad, what does he think about this?
    If he doesn't love you
Please know that I do
    If you give me a chance
I'll show you.
    You'll make mistakes and I will too
But we'll have each other to cry to.
    Don't worry about your life. Put it in
God's hands, he'll know what to do.
    That's my promise to you
The first time you hold me in your arms
    You'll know my life was meant to be
God created me,
    And he chose you to be my mommy

My Own

I only want to fall in love
        If the love is true
It has been my experience
        That love can hurt you
Leaving you with painful scars
        That can never be erased
Or happy memories that cannot be traced
        The love you felt was
Real, now it has come to the point that you
        Can no longer feel
Love, how can it be, it's all I ever wanted
        and now look at me
Broken hearted and all alone, with no one
        To call my own

Trapped

I have some anger and pain
   That I need to let out
It's trapped inside
   And I can't get it out
Feelings of loneliness, heartache, and despair
   Is there a God
Please help me if you're out there
   Misplaced hate
   Superficial love
If I don't get it out
   I fear I won't make it through the gate
I cry inside but no one seems to hear me
   Where is the care and the love that has never
surrounded me?
Left here alone to die
   No one ever to hearing my voice
Or asking the question why
   Your lack of concern
Has assisted in my suicide
I have some anger and pain
   That I need to let out
I fear it's too late
   And me you will have to do without

My Best

I should have let you love me
   But instead I let you slip away
I sit and contemplate what we have been today
   You told me you loved me
And offered to give me the world
   Instead I trampled your heart
Not knowing I was crushing my world
   Things are different
I've found love
   But it's not true
I long for the happiness that I felt
   Every time I was with you
When I'm still I can hear my heart cry
   And a faint whisper
     That asks why
My heart is divided
   My soul is not at rest
I now realize while I was with you
   I was at my best

One Last Kiss

You promised me forever
    You said you would never leave
You broke my heart
    And left it there to bleed
Without notice
    Not even one last kiss
It was the grand finale
    And I was dismissed
A single tear remains in my eye
    And a permanent scar that reads "why"
My life will never be the same
    And my pain will remain
You promised me forever
    And said I was yours to keep
Instead you tossed me out into the
    Deep blue sea
As I sank to the ocean's floor
    And hit rock bottom
I thought to myself
    I can live without him
I opened my eyes
    And was given one last breath
I gained momentum as I swam to the top
    My pain will remain
But I will not stop

My journey is far from over
And I have persevered
Don't offer me one last kiss
And don't ever call me dear

Please Let Me Love You

Please let me love you and show you
What all I can be
Please let me love you so that you can
See a deeper side of me
Please let me love you so you can
See that I am true
Please let me love you, I promise
I won't forsake you
Please let me love you
The way you need to be loved
Please let me love you
You're all I truly think of
Please let me love you
It would mean so much to me
Once you do, you will see
What you are searching for in man
Is only found in me.

I Love You

I love you for who you are
      No matter what you do.
For some strange reason
      My heart won't let go of you.
Through mountains and valleys we've traveled,
      But my love stands unshaken and
        Grows deeper too.
Our souls are one, united we will stand
      Love will have the upper hand
For all that you say, and all that you do
      Love will conquer all, even that
        Loveless side of you.
Close to my heart you'll always be
Me loving you and eventually you loving me too.
You are my world and will always be
      That significant part that completes me
When you are ready and not a minute before,
      Love will greet you at the front door.
You will come in, we'll sit down and dine
      And we will forget about old times.
We'll focus on our present, and where to go

From here, now that love is dwelling here
While I'm still breathing please hold me near
For this moment in time will never reappear.
We'll make it last forever, I know, because this
Is true love, the only love that I ever
Want to know

Mystical

Mystical beauty

       Deep within his soul

As I gazed intently

       His eyes contain a story

That has yet to be told

       His whisper touches the most

Delicate parts of my naked soul

       Longing to be touched

I have to be careful

Because his passionate masculinity

May be too much

       Who creates such a man

That a woman has yet to know

       That has the ability

To make her insides explode

       Who is he

Why does his love run so deep?

       Every part of him

Is a treasure to keep

So, what is the connection

Will I ever be his to keep

His mystical beauty

Will remain a mystery to me

Today he said some beautiful things

      That penetrated my soul

His word caressed me in a way

      That soothes my aching

I desire to taste his love

      To inhale his being

Was he sent to me to set me free

      To let my love run wild with him

Will he see all that I am

or will he search to find me

      Does he hold the key

To unlock my broken heart

      Or will he be a stent that failed to repair it

His love is toxic

      I desire to drown in his affection

      To be captivated by his love

Is it authentic? I must ask myself this question

Will I be able to embrace

What I fear is mine

Or will I wander aimlessly through time

Searching for someone who will never be mine

Awake My Love

Love awakened before its time
       Is dangerous
Because the one who awakens it
       May not be mine
The virgin heart is frail
       Ready to love without judgement
       Ready to run free
       Not tamed by the past
       It only lives for the moment
It can be a bit brash
       Or exactly what you need it to be
Love awakened before it's time
       Has dreadful consequences
It says love me now
       Let's defy time
Know it has awoken
       Will you still be mine

Her

She sat at the table staring at her phone

Alone again, table for one

This was no coincidence

And it's starting not to be fun

She possessed something extraordinary

Like rays of energy similar to the sun

When you look at her you can't help but to stare

It was more than her beauty

It was her uniqueness

And my, was it rare

Should I inquire

Do I dare

It was something deep on the inside

That I needed to see

Then it would all make sense, this unfathomable mystery

Could she be the one in my dreams?

Silly me, things are never what they seem

She turned and caught my stare

This woman was powerful

I had to turn my head

I couldn't stare

I wanted so badly to ask her name

But I couldn't work up the courage

She left

And I remained

Him

As I sat alone, dinner reserved for one
I reflected on life and all I've done
What did I do to get here and what work needs to be done?
Another question that comes to mind
Is why haven't I found him
Where is he
When will I know if he is the one
With the blink of an eye
A handsome young man walked by and said hi
He said, "You're here all alone, may I ask why?"
I said "You see, I am a child of the most high
I'm waiting on some things.
I've asked
And I'm waiting for reply."
The young man stared intently in my eyes
He said, "I want to hear about these things,
please tell me more."
I went on to tell him about my purpose and
How God was beginning to open up doors
He said, "May I pause you? I have to get this out.
The Lord told me to tell you I'm yours"
Not knowing what to say
Tears began to fall from my eyes
He gently wiped them and said
"I am here now. You will not need to cry
I've been looking for you

most of my life too.

But I was scared to trust God

And was delayed in finding you.

See, we have a purpose

And we are going to be blessed

God has not forgotten what he promised

Which is why he put us through many tests.

To whom much is given much is required.

The gifts he's placed in us

Will take his kingdom higher.

I think you've had enough

That's all you can withstand

We will take it step-by-step

And together we will conquer the land.

You are my future.

I will never let you go.

I promise to love and protect you.

He will bless us

And show us how to love and grow."

By now I realized this wasn't a dream

He was real

I had met my King.

Goodbye

I have to say goodbye
As these tears are profusely streaming from my eyes
My heart is fragile
>It easily comes undone

Love has taken place
>And it seems that it has won

The loudest whisper
The faintest cry
All at once
My emotions
I cannot hide
Everything I'm made of
>You lack the ability to actually see

If you did
>You would hold on tightly to me

You made me feel special
Yet you didn't handle me with care
All I wanted was for you to come to love me
I honestly thought you would always be there
It was you who I wanted to adore
>I'm drowning in agony

>Waiting to be washed up on the shore

Will the love in me ever be restored?
>With each passing moment

>I wither away even more

History repeats itself

At least that's what they say

       This is more like a recurring nightmare

       That won't go away

How did I get here?

       Why am I made like this?

I have to say goodbye

       I am a treasure

       One that you will surely start to miss

I Let Him In

I stand here paralyzed

His talons have pierced my heart

My greatest fear is taking them out

I fear if I let go

I will have to walk in the unknown

What will wait on the other side for me?

     More pain

     Perhaps prolonged misery

I have to find a way to escape

One that won't make me regret this day

     I let him in

Now look, I'm staring at my end

How did I get here?

     Where does this come from

     will love be held hostage

     until I'm done

My beauty is irrelevant

My talents hold no meaning

My value is insignificant

Where did I find you?

That's the problem, you see

I found you

You didn't find me

The pain from your talons

Will forever remain in me

The Necklace

He gave me a necklace
That had power inside
The joy of love
He clothed me in the finest
And gave me diamonds and pearls
I was his little secret
One kept well hidden
From the rest of the world
He gave me the illusion
That he was mine to keep
But deep inside the lies ran deep
The freedom I once felt when I laid
In his arms
Was tainted by the truth that
Was revealed when I gazed intently
In his eyes
How will I recover
All that remains is pain

Loving You

I wanted you to love me
I needed you so bad
You are the best that I ever had
You caressed my mind
And penetrated my soul
I lost myself in you
I thought we would grow old
I'm left with another sad story
This is getting old
What is it about me
That is not getting told
Broken hearted I stand here today
loving you
As you walk away......

He Was Beautiful

He was beautiful

His presence pierced my heart

Love was in his eyes

But I question his heart

When I am with him my wounds are healed

I feel his love and it feels so real

Do I fall in his love?

Or flee after the moment

My love

My emotions

I can hardly hold them in

Do I trust chance

And let love come in

Love is a journey that may never be won

But if I never give it a chance

I won't experience the warmth and its fun

They say it's better to have loved

Than to not love at all

Will I take a chance?

And let love conquer all

A Single Tear

A single tear remains in my eye
I'm mourning a lost love
While he is still here
But why
Could it be what happened yesterday
Or do I fear what might take place today
Trust is earned
Still no promise is guaranteed
What will happen
Depends on a lot of things
Where is God
What is his plan
Or did he leave it to me
And place it in my hands
Time is of no value
It too makes mistakes
It fails to show up sooner
Too late, utter ruin
Detriment has taken place
Life is a lesson
And we all must learn
But we have to take chances
And maybe one day we will get
What we think we've earned

He Let Me Slip Away

He let me slip away

But why

Once again

I'm left with tears streaming from my eyes

Why does this happen

What mistakes did I make?

Time and time again

       Am I impatient

       Why can't I wait

They always love me

So, they say

Then after I'm gone

They realize they've made a mistake

They admit they were wrong

And resort to blaming fate

       Who is fate and where did it come into play

       Furthermore, why is she allowed to dictate

       Well it appears she has the final say

I'm left powerless

And my source of energy

Has let me slip away

I can't help but yell

Why in God's name

They Say I'm Beautiful

They say I'm beautiful, but what does that really mean
I still continue to chase love and dream wild dreams
Does beauty mend brokenness
Or promise a life well lived
Does beauty give back
After I have given all I have left to give
I ask one question
Will beauty set me free
Will it protect me from this inner turmoil deep inside of me
Beauty means nothing as it has the ability to age away
When it does, what do I have left
What can you say
They say I'm beautiful, but what does that mean
If you fail to recognize the deeper beauty inside of me

Naked

He warms my heart
He makes me smile
Beauty is all he sees
My flaws are no longer a part of me
Who am I
Do I deserve such love?
This love has set me free
Free from worry
Free from perfection
Free from everything that has bound me
I'm bare
I lay naked
Who is this man
Maybe it's his heart
Maybe it's a higher power
That had this planned from the start
He has given me something beautiful
Something that I will always feel
His love
Yes, I know it's real

The Bookstore

The bookstore
Is this where I will find him
My one true love

Is he a lover of books?
Was he sent from above
This silly game I play
What's the purpose?
I believe it's fading away

I looked for you
I made myself available
What's the use?

Lonely I shall remain
I fear I will never be claimed
Where is this man
I don't hear you calling
Aren't I your dame

Oh, silly girl
This is a shame
He's not in this bookstore
I'm so glad you came
But please, miss, stop calling his name

Bleeding Heart

His talons gripped me and induced great fear
His toxic love
Makes all I've ever known disappear
I tried to pry them out
Out of sheer fear
His love was so strong
I've succumbed to injury
My greatest fear
There's no tomorrow
There's no way out
The end is here

Heartbreak

This man gone break my heart
Why did I ignore the signs?
I seen them from the start
Could it be my thirst for love?

Why the lack of patience?
Why can't I trust God with my love?
I try and try again
No matter what I do
I can't win

Such beauty within my soul
But goes unnoticed
Which is why this same story keeps getting told
I give up
This is way past old

Not This Time

Maybe it was easier for him not to say goodbye
I sit here now, tears won't even fall from my eye
With a sober heart I can't help but to ask why
This time I thought it was real
Something I would enjoy
Something I would always feel
Detach the strings that connect our hearts
So I don't bleed when he decides to leave
Not this time
Love won't be the death of me......

Loving Me

I've fallen in love with her
She's beautiful, talented and gifted
She is everything I ever wanted to be
In fact, she has always lived inside of me
It just took me some time to see
Now that I have her
I will treasure her and help her grow
She will be my first love
I will never let her go

My Heart

Suspended in time
Hold me gently
Your body pressed against mine
My love is fragile
Only to grow with time
My mind so deep
Conception will only take place
With the one who has the key
Suspended in time
My heart beats no more
I no longer have to search
love has found me
And this time, it said **to me**

I'm yours

Permission To Love

Will his affection be for me
And mine for him
Do I have permission to love him
Before it's time
Who is time that he waits on a man
Does infinity long to be free
Happily ever after, are those words for me
Search the depths of my soul
Prepare me for love
Make me whole

Love

How I wish I had a summer love
Oh, how time would fly
You would love me every day that passes by
You would hold me in your arms at night
And awaken me gently with the kiss
In the morning's light
I would dream wild dreams
And you would make them come true
I finally found someone I can trust and it's you
Forever in my heart you will always be
Remember this line, please for me
For this season is changing
And the leaves are falling fast
Our love will fade
Because we don't have what it takes to make it last
As we depart
I'll wipe the tears from my eyes
And leave you my heart
I know in time we will both see
That summer love is only temporary.

Aftershocks

I lay here

Emotions bare

What is life that mine should be protected

Will my heart give way

Or will it change its rhythm

Will love kill me

Or become a fleeting thought

Aftershocks I can feel throughout my heart

Perhaps it was the trauma

I ask myself, "Will I ever heal?"

Victory was never mine

It was a tool to control me and leave me blind

Absence from life

I will not miss

I lay here

Questioning the purpose of all of this

Love Why

Why does love make me weary
Why does it have to make so many mistakes?
It's made to be gentle
And take my breath away
It's supposed to wipe my tears
And understand my cries
It stays and work things out
And it refuses to say Goodbye
All that love is made of, I cannot comprehend
It can be your worst enemy
Or yet, your very best friend
Love shouldn't be complicated
Yet so many meet their demise
Love's cunning
It drips seduction
And alters what you see with your eyes
It snatches you
And immediately you're whisked away
You will never be the same
Once love has had its way

In My Heart Alone

In my heart I'm alone

      I search for meaning

            Beyond my given identity

I go through the motions

      But love is far from my heart

A single tear runs down my face

      My story? Where do I start?

My journey alone

      Or that pain I cannot disown

Maybe it's the love

      That I've never experienced

Wait, it's the friendships

      That all abruptly ended

Peace I do not know

      Darkness has embraced me so

Where did it start

      When will it end

I'm searching for answers

      Is there not one

Who will soothe my soul

before my life is done

      I'm crying out

This is beyond my control

No one will help

I'm all alone

Beyond The Deep

All of me loved you

> For you I would die

I lay here motionless

> Asking myself why

What we had was real

> Our love, nothing could kill

Warm summer nights

> The passionate kiss we shared

Under the moonlight

You touched me gently, never

Violating my volatile soul

> Flames of fire burning deep in my soul

To feel like this every day till we grow old

> All of you loved me

But hidden was a secret

> You longed to keep

Your flames burned

> But not for a woman like me

That song you wrote

> You will never again sing for me

With you she will grow old

She is the one you will hold

You have traveled far beyond the deep

You are no longer mine to keep

While I lay here motionless

I asked myself why.

Search Within

I'm searching for something that I cannot find

      A love that will surpass the limits of time

I ask myself

      Does such a love exist

Why was I created

      To feel such bliss

A longing deep inside

      I cannot even visualize

Who will go to that place to love me

      They must first share my pain

To merely know me, is not to love me

      Shallow love will never find me

It goes beyond an intimate kiss

      Just because you call me beautiful

Doesn't mean I'm ready to be your Mrs.

      Broken inside

Fragments of a puzzle

      I can no longer hide

Who is he

      Who fails to search inside?

True love will see

     Past the many layers of me

and learn to love me, ever so carefully, then I

will stop searching for what I can't find,

because I will *have met a love,*

     that surpasses the limits of time.

Speak To My Heart

Speak to my heart, Lord, for I'm in the midst of a trial

Sometimes I fear that I might be here for a while.

If this is your will, then let it be so

But, please speak to my heart so I'll

Know which way to go

Whatever you decide will be all right with me

As long as this is the path that you have chosen for me.

I might not like it or even understand,

But if this is your will,

I will obey every command

For in time

I will see

All of the changes you are trying to make in me

Speak to my heart to give me comfort and peace

For what I am battling is much bigger than me

Sometimes I feel

That I cannot withstand

The pressure that I experience

From this task at hand

I've come this far and made it through

Only because I have trusted in you.

Please give me strength

And encourage me too

So that I may run this race,

The whole way through.

Victorious I will be at the end of this journey

But I must not try to finish it early

For if I try, my plans won't succeed

And I will mess up God's plan indeed.

As I quieted my soul, you spoke to my heart

Now I know where I must start

I have to be still

And learn patience too,

Because both of these leads to virtue.

These are the things you are requiring of me.

Lord, please help me be content,

Content with thee

Only You

I look at you

        And see what my life should have been

Where happiness and intimacy has no end

        A place where love never sleeps

I could give you my heart and let you

        Travel to the deep

Ever so vulnerable I would be

A question of faithfulness would never come to mind

Security in your arms at all times

        You would be my armor

And bear all of my pain

        With you I would never worry

Because you would always be there

Is it too late for me to be with someone like you?

Where the sky has no limits

        And it will always be blue

For as long as I live

        you will always have a part of me

Reserved only for you.

    The next time I look at you

It will be real

    I will no longer have to wonder

Because I will feel

    And be secure because this love is real.

Forever Yours

Forever yours I told myself I would
      Be, for all eternity
I would be the first and the last to
      Love you so true
My heart, my world and my life
      Is you.
There's no one that can compare to you
      Because of the rare beauty that is
         Found only in you
I love you and forever will, this you can
      Believe because it's real
I have given you a part of me
      This you will always feel
May our love be beautiful until time
Stands still

Bare Skin

He asked her to give him her heart

In exchange for his world

He promised her happily ever after

And told her she would always be his girl

So, she bared her skin

And let all of her love flow out from within

That soon ended, it was no longer bliss

The arrangement was over

She had her final kiss

Although she wanted to cry

Remembering

The first day he said hi

She didn't want to live her life believing this is what
love feels like

With her bare skin she vowed to love again

And be someone's dream

This time he would truly love her

And she would forever be his Queen

Second Chance

If I could have another chance at life, I would

I would avoid the same mistakes and know it was for my good

I would kiss his lips and softly whisper goodbye

I would not turn back, I would let my heart cry

And ignore that inner voice that asks why

I would walk with confidence and not question the unknown

I would live life as if time was something that I owned

I would never do anything in haste

and never on my own

I would let someone love me

But only when it was time

I wouldn't question his sincerity

Because I would know that he's mine

I would live life to the fullest

And forever be at my best

I would shine like the sun

And bless others with my presence

I would quickly forgive others

For everyone makes mistakes

I would love deeply

no conditions would apply

I would embrace freedom

And wipe the tears from my eyes

If I had a second chance I would

Be the agent of change

and embrace the good . . . .

Queen

I'm a Queen
Treasured and highly esteemed
I won't settle for less because I'm
Somebody's dream
My Mind
My Heart
My Inner beauty
Where do I start
My conception is a mystery
His anointing runs so deep it can
Annihilate history
I'm like nothing you've ever seen
No more chasing fantasies
I will help you live out your dreams
Without me things fall apart
Because I stem from God's heart
Who am I
A Queen, to be highly treasured and
Always esteemed

Table For One

Table for one again
she might be alone today
But not forever, she has found her soul mate

She thought her loneliness was over
In fact, it was just the beginning
Was this a mistake?

She experienced him in a way
That would ensure a happy ending
Was this a mistake?

What she didn't know
Was he was not yet hers to keep
She would have to walk through the storm
To prove that the love was deep

She questioned God
Why would you do this to me
Give me a treasure that I cannot keep

I've waited so long
To have someone I can call my own
I'm thinking why
As I sit all alone

I want him
And he wants me
I have to be patient, just wait and see

He is faithful, I will see
And when its time
You will release him to me
Deep in love
And one we shall be

Thank You

I hope you have enjoyed me sharing my heart. It is my hope that if you are looking for love, you will find it. Be patient, love takes time. I would also like to thank you for buying or downloading my book, it means a lot to me. I hope I have touched your heart in some way. It is imperative that you provide me with feedback about my book. I am looking for an honest review. Please leave a review or feedback. This is important as it will allow me to improve as a writer.

Ways to connect with me:

Email: connect@loveariston.com
Or visit my website: LoveAriston.com
And of course, I'm on social media.
Facebook – Ariston CM
Twitter & Instagram - ImSoAriston
Hugs & Kisses, Ariston!

Acknowledgements

First, I would like to thank God, the Almighty Creator, for walking this path called life with me. It has not been an easy journey, but without His grace and mercy I don't know where I would be. While I don't understand everything about God I am grateful for His love.

I am so grateful for my SPS community who was there every time I needed something. I would like to thank everyone that assisted me in making this book great, from start to finish. No matter how small your contribution was, it was most appreciated. I would like to thank my former accountability partner who I am so happy to now call my friend.

I would like to thank my children who always adapt to our ever-changing lives. Everything I do, I do it for all of you. You all mean so much to me and I love you with all my heart. I am so happy to have all of you.

Finally, I would like to thank my right hand, R.L.D. for all her dedication and loyalty to the cause. Thank you for your morning calls and endless encouragement. I would not stay on task if it were not for you. Love you, girl!

Please forgive me, as there were others not mentioned that assisted me in some form or fashion Thanks, love you, guys!

About the Author

Ariston C.M. was born in Ohio. Today she is a single mother of five, living in Ohio. She is an entrepreneur. She holds multiple degrees in theology and child development. Her challenges as a child ultimately inspired her to start a non-profit organization that currently addresses the needs of at-risk youth and those with developmental disabilities. In her free time, she writes poetry and participates in speaking engagements that empower women in all sectors of life, but with particular dedication to survivors like herself. Through telling her story she hopes to shatter the barriers all women face, from society and themselves.

www.ingramcontent.com/pod-product-compliance
Lightning Source LLC
Chambersburg PA
CBHW071631040426
42452CB00009B/1581